A FULL-LENGTH PLAY

Was He Anyone?

by

N. F. SIMPSON

9780571102709
AF571937

THE DRAMATIC PUBLISHING COMPANY
CHICAGO

NOTICE

The royalty fees for this play are $35.00 for the first amateur performance and $25.00 for the second, providing arrangements are made in advance. Royalty must be paid whether the play is presented for charity or profit and whether admission is charged or not. *A play is performed any time it is acted before an audience.*

COPYRIGHT LAW GIVES THE AUTHOR OR HIS AGENT THE EXCLUSIVE RIGHT TO MAKE COPIES.

This law provides authors with a fair return for their creative efforts. Authors earn their living from the royalties they receive on the book sale and on the performance of their works. To copy parts or give performances of a royalty play without paying royalties robs the authors of their livelihood.

Conscientious observance of the Copyright Law is not only ethical, it encourages authors to continue their creative work. *It is dishonest and illegal to copy parts or perform a royalty play without advance permission.*

The amateur stage rights are available on the above terms, which are subject to change without notice. All other rights are reserved. On all programs this notice should appear: Produced by arrangement with THE DRAMATIC PUBLISHING COMPANY, of Chicago.

© MCMLXXIII By
N.F. SIMPSON
Printed in the United States of America
All Rights Reserved
[WAS HE ANYONE ?]

WAS HE ANYONE?

A Full Length Play

For Three Men and Four Women*

CHARACTERS

MR. WILLIAMS . . . . . . (Mr. Burbage, Clarence, Archbishop, Cabinet Minister, T.V. Director)

MR. VERNON . . . . (Mr. Baverstock, Senior Civil Servant, Mr. Clapton, Piano Engineer, Production Assistant)

MR. PUTNEY . . . (Steward, Junior Civil Servant, Solicitor, Trade Union Leader, Lawyer, Interviewer)

SYBIL . . . . . . (Miss Rugg, Mrs. Clacton, Mrs. Treplatchly, Mrs. Dubarge)

MISS STEWART . . . . (Mrs. Crabbe-Harmsworth, Mrs. Carthage, Mrs. Blithehampton)

MISS HUGHES . . . (Miss Havergal, Flagselling Lady, Miss Linthropp, Second Employee, Girl Reporter, Receptionist Nun, Trainee)

MRS. WHITBRACE

PLACE: *Here and there.*

TIME: *The present.*

*Cast may be expanded by eliminating the doubling.

Scene 1

(A voice offstage is heard making the following announcement:)

National Help-You-Out Year Week Campaign. We exist, as you know, to give help to all who are in difficulties wherever they may be. In thanking you for your generous support in past years, may I appeal to you for your continued cooperation in bringing to our notice all those known to you who may be in trouble . . . whether it be a brother-in-law who has disappeared without trace down a tin mine, a favorite aunt who has been towed away on a camel in the Sahara, a husband whose shoe laces have become entangled in the undergrowth in some tropical jungle, or merely an absent-minded explorer who has got himself totally lost in the middle of nowhere and is desperate for the kind of help we are so well equipped to give . . .

LIGHTS start to come up on a poster which reads:

National Help-You-Out Year Week.

LIGHTS come up further and we are in a small nondescript room in a house, which has been converted into a one-man office with trestle table and other paraphernalia appropriate to a small home-based campaign that is beginning to expand. MR. WILLIAMS comes in wearing outdoor clothes and carrying some letters.

He takes off his overcoat and hangs it up. He is followed by MR. VERNON, who has been in the office for some time.

VERNON (in the middle of conversation). Totally lost in the middle of nowhere, so we did the obvious thing.
WILLIAMS. And flew a map out to him. Only to discover . . .
VERNON. That he didn't know how to read it.
WILLIAMS (preoccupied with a letter). So what . . . ?
VERNON. Well . . . it meant flying him home at enormous expense for map-reading classes, and then the minute he gets back there what does he do? Goes striding off into the sunset with his nose in an atlas and falls straight over the edge of a precipice.
WILLIAMS. Wasn't marked, I suppose.
VERNON. Why should it be? You're expected to keep your eyes open.
WILLIAMS (looking at another letter). Yes.
VERNON. Anyway, there he is . . . dangling in mid-air from a gorsebush . . . which means we've got to send him out a set of encyclopedias or something to keep his mind occupied while we get some sort of rescue organized.
WILLIAMS. Well . . . there it is. That's what National Help-You-Out Year Week's all about.
VERNON. Yes. I suppose it is.
WILLIAMS. In the meantime, what's being done about . . . oh . . .

(BARBARA HUGHES enters.)

MISS HUGHES. A Mrs. Whitbrace.
WILLIAMS. What does she want?
MISS HUGHES. It's about her husband. Could we

help out at all?

WILLIAMS. You'd better send her in.

MISS HUGHES. Yes. (BARBARA HUGHES exits.)

VERNON (picking up pamphlets). You were going to ask me about these.

WILLIAMS (taking them). Ah. They've come. (Reading from title page.) "Cries For Help Through the Ages and How They Have Been Answered."

VERNON. Five hundred. At fifty new pence each.

WILLIAMS. Good.

(MISS HUGHES shows MRS. WHITBRACE in.)

WILLIAMS. Mrs. Whitbrace? Worried about your husband, I gather.

MRS. WHITBRACE. That's right.

MISS HUGHES. She says she was sent here from the Welfare.

WILLIAMS. What better place to come to?

(MISS STEWART enters.)

WILLIAMS. Just the thing for Miss Stewart, by the sound of it. (To MISS STEWART.) This is Mrs. . . .

MRS. WHITBRACE. Whitbrace.

WILLIAMS. Mrs. Whitbrace. Problem with regard to her husband.

MISS STEWART. Oh. Is he here?

MRS. WHITBRACE. Well, no. He's . . . he's not.

MISS STEWART. Where is he?

MRS. WHITBRACE. He's in the Mediterranean. (MISS STEWART gives her a weighing-up sort of look.)

MISS STEWART. When you say in the Mediterranean . . .

MRS. WHITBRACE. Well . . .
MISS HUGHES. You mean actually _in_.
MRS. WHITBRACE. All except his _head_.
WILLIAMS. And that's above water.
MRS. WHITBRACE. So far it is, yes. Touch wood. (Pause as they take this in.) He goes under from time to time, but . . .
MISS STEWART. On the whole . . .
MRS. WHITBRACE. On the whole, it's . . .
MISS STEWART. Yes. How did this . . . happen? . . .
MISS HUGHES. He fell overboard . . . I think . . .
MRS. WHITBRACE. Yes. He's a bookmaker's runner, you see.
MISS HUGHES. She feels she should have warned him.
MISS STEWART. Warned him of what?
MRS. WHITBRACE. Well, he takes a pride in his work, and . . . he was on this . . . cargo boat . . . and he woke up in the night. (To MISS STEWART it is the familiar old story.)
MISS STEWART (finishing her story for her). Forgot where he was, broke into a trot from force of habit, and straight off the end of the boat and into the . . . (She pushes a tape recorder button. Loud cry, hugh splash, shout of "Man overboard." There is a moment or two of slightly bemused silence.)
MRS. WHITBRACE. He's known professionally as Greased Lightning, you see. On account of the speed he goes at, when he's running. (MISS STEWART is the first to gather herself together.)
MISS STEWART. Bookmaker's runner . . . on board a cargo boat several sizes too small for him . . . I suppose it's something of an occupational hazard . . . though what one can be expected to do about it . . .
WILLIAMS. Perhaps we could hear the . . . (Vague

gesture toward tape recorder, glance into wings.) . . . again. (Loud cry, huge splash, shout of "Man overboard.") Yes. (Bemused pause.) It looks to me slightly as though we might be in a better position to sort this one out if we took a look at the situation from somewhat closer quarters.

MISS STEWART. Yes. I think a Mediterranean cruise might well be the answer.

MISS HUGHES. Yes, I think it would.

WILLIAMS. Perhaps, Mr. Vernon . . .

VERNON. Yes. I'll put it in hand. (He picks up the telephone and makes a call.)

WILLIAMS (to MRS. WHITBRACE). Once we've sized up the situation at first hand, we can take steps to get the machinery moving.

MRS. WHITBRACE. Oh, well, thank you. I'd be ever so grateful if you could.

WILLIAMS. Put a fairly substantial rocket behind the powers that be, with a view to getting the whole thing referred forward with the minimum delay. In that way we can have him out of the water for you at the earliest possible moment.

MRS. WHITBRACE. It's his lifejacket, you see. It's getting waterlogged.

WILLIAMS. Yes. (VERNON puts telephone down.)

VERNON. It seems there's a cruise liner there already.

MISS STEWART. Fly out and join it.

VERNON. I rather fancy it's fully booked up.

MISS STEWART. One can but try. (They disperse.)

BLACKOUT

Scene 2

LIGHTS come up on a small luxury cruise liner. Early morning. Upstage is a ship's rail. Visible "S.S. Bay of Naples" on a lifebelt. View across calm, blue sea to bay of Naples. Sunshine, sound of water lapping and of ropes gently straining and creaking, and occasionally the cry of seagulls. Idyllic peace.

Downstage is the ship's dining room. Some of the ship's passengers are: a middle-aged, slightly country couple who address each other as CLARENCE (played by Mr. Williams) and SYBIL respectively; a Knightsbridge lady named MRS. CRABBE-HARMSWORTH (played by Miss Stewart), accompanied by her companion, MISS ELSPETH HAVERGAL (played by Miss Hughes).

We hear a thin, distant cry of "Heeeeeelp! Heeeeeeeelp!"

MR. PUTNEY, strolling round the deck, and MISS HAVERGAL, on her way to breakfast, encounter one another. MISS HAVERGAL stops, shy and in two minds, and then speaks.

MISS HAVERGAL. What a perfect idyllic day!
PUTNEY. Isn't it?
MISS HAVERGAL. Just the mewing of the seagulls.
PUTNEY. Heavenly. (MISS HAVERGAL goes down. MR. PUTNEY goes off.)
VOICE (offstage). Heeeeeeelp! Heeeeeeelp!

(CLARENCE, SYBIL, MRS. CRABBE-HARMSWORTH and MISS HAVERGAL enter the dining room and go to their tables. CLARENCE and SYBIL are sitting at one table, and MRS. CRABBE-HARMSWORTH and MISS HAVERGAL are at another table.)

SYBIL. Four o'clock this morning.

MRS. CRABBE-HARMSWORTH. Yes. We were woken by it.

SYBIL. Who is it? Does anyone know?

MRS. CRABBE-HARMSWORTH. It's not one of ours, I'm pleased to say, but apart from that it could be anyone.

SYBIL. You'd think it might occur to somebody to send a lifeboat. (They address themselves to the task of what to order for breakfast.)

VOICE (offstage). Help! Help! (Decision made, they turn to *The Times*.) Help! Help!

SYBIL. I see from *The Times* that dear Lord Farnborough is giving one of his balls for charity.

MRS. CRABBE-HARMSWORTH. They say it's the last one. (Pause.)

VOICE (offstage). Help! Help! (MISS HAVERGAL glances toward the open porthole.)

MISS HAVERGAL. Should I . . . ?

MRS. CRABBE-HARMSWORTH. I think one of us should do something, Elspeth.

MISS HAVERGAL (gets up). Yes. I'll just . . . (She crosses to porthole.) . . . shut some of it out, at any rate. (MISS HAVERGAL closes porthole.)

MRS. CRABBE-HARMSWORTH. Within reason is one thing.

SYBIL. Well, quite.

MRS. CRABBE-HARMSWORTH. If one hasn't got the message now, one isn't going to.

MISS HAVERGAL (looking out porthole). They seem to have provided him with a raft.

MRS. CRABBE-HARMSWORTH. Which he was sitting on, if you please, when I came down.

SYBIL. Sitting on?

MRS. CRABBE-HARMSWORTH. Hardly the purpose, one would have thought, for which it was intended.

SYBIL. I should think not.

CLARENCE. Laxness on the part of the powers that be, I suppose. All too ready to turn a blind eye. As long as he satisfies certain minimum requirements so far as being deemed a drowning person within the meaning of the Act is concerned . . . that's all that matters.

(MISS HAVERGAL exits. SENIOR CIVIL SERVANT /played by Mr. Vernon/ crosses upstage ramp accompanied by JUNIOR CIVIL SERVANT /played by Putney/ as though along Whitehall corridor. Lights dim down on dining room area and come up on SENIOR and JUNIOR CIVIL SERVANT as they walk along ramp, deep in discussion.)

SENIOR. Some part of him in contact with the water at all times. That's the crucial thing.

JUNIOR. Dangling his feet through a hole in the middle.

SENIOR. Done reasonably discreetly, and not in such a way as to draw overt attention to it.

JUNIOR. He seems to be behaving with a certain amount of common-sense in the matter.

SENIOR. Good. And otherwise to be used solely as a servicing platform and general storage area for food, change of clothing, reading matter and so on.

JUNIOR. That's in hand.

SENIOR. With Elsan.

JUNIOR (takes out a notebook and makes a note). Ah.

SENIOR. Calls of nature. He'll need that.

JUNIOR. Red warning light for the use of shipping at night, and the usual marker buoys . . . although I should imagine he's become sufficient of a landmark by now for that to be largely a formality.

SENIOR. And let's hope he's not there all that much longer. (They go off. Lights dim down on ramp area and come up on dining area again.)

CLARENCE. Move afoot to have him brought up on board, so someone was saying.

MRS. CRABBE-HARMSWORTH. No! Surely not.

CLARENCE. It's a bit . . .

MRS. CRABBE-HARMSWORTH. I should think it was!

CLARENCE. Nice enough chap and all that, I dare say, but . . .

SYBIL. Embarrassing for him . . . embarrassing for everyone else.

(FLAG-SELLING LADY appears /played by Miss Hughes/. BAVERSTOCK /played by Mr. Vernon/ enters dining room and sits at one of the tables.)

FLAG-SELLER (coming into dining room and addressing group). Good morning. I hope it's not too early to start accosting people, but . . . so many demands on one's purse these days . . . I'm always afraid if I don't get in first . . . Thank you so much . . . (Pins flag on BAVERSTOCK.)

BAVERSTOCK. What's it for, this time?

FLAG-SELLER. It's for the potholers. Trapped in the Andes. To provide pocket chess sets and things, and table tennis equipment, to help pass the time while they're waiting for things to be sorted out at the United Nations . . .

VOICE (offstage). Heeeeeeelp! Heeeeeeelp!

FLAG-SELLER. I wonder . . . do you think? . . . (Calling through open porthole.) World National Help-You-Out Year Week! We're collecting for potholers trapped in the Andes! (To those at the tables.) He seems not to be taking any notice.

CLARENCE. Too preoccupied with shouting for help.

BAVERSTOCK. Vary the tone occasionally; it might be a bit more acceptable.

FLAG-SELLER (trying to call out porthole again). World National Help-You-Out Year Week! (To those at table.) He seems to be making some kind of sign, but it's too far away to be certain what it is. One can just make out two fingers, and that's all.

CLARENCE. Probably trying to indicate that he's got no change on him.

FLAG-SELLER. Perhaps one should ask to be rowed out to him. One would hate him to feel he was being left out simply because he's in trouble.

CLARENCE. I think you might find when you got out there that he contributes privately.

FLAG-SELLER. Such a pity if he were to feel one's only interested in people who are comfortably off.

(She takes off the Salvation Army bonnet, ditches the flag tray, sits down again and reverts to being MISS HAVERGAL.)

BAVERSTOCK. Indefatigable.

SYBIL. Isn't she?

BAVERSTOCK. Good causes'd be lost without her. (Pause.) Interesting subject. Giving. And what motivates people.

MRS. CRABBE-HARMSWORTH. We never give, as a rule. On principle.

SYBIL. No. We hardly ever do.

MRS. CRABBE-HARMSWORTH. Except to the one or two we give to regularly.

SYBIL. It so quickly becomes meaningless.

VOICE (offstage). Heeeelp! Heeelp!

BAVERSTOCK. Appeals for this, appeals for that. You'd never stop.

SYBIL. Exactly. (Pause.)

MRS. CRABBE-HARMSWORTH. Not that some of them aren't very good, of course. In the way they're done. On the wireless particularly. There are some very good appeals for this or that charity, if you happen to have it on sometimes, at the appropriate moment.

CLARENCE. Sundays, in particular.

MISS HAVERGAL. What was that very moving appeal we heard last Sunday?

SYBIL. Oh, did you hear that, too? So did we. (To CLARENCE.) What was it for? Surely you remember.

CLARENCE. Yes, I'm trying to remember.

MISS HAVERGAL. We sat there, didn't we, afterwards.

SYBIL. Yes. We sat there for a good ten minutes before either of us could say a word. I don't know when we've been so completely knocked out by an appeal. What _was_ it for?

CLARENCE. It was one of the best they've ever done.

VOICE (offstage). Heeeeeeelp! Heeeeeeelp!

BAVERSTOCK. The way it's put over, of course.

SYBIL. Oh, absolutely.

BAVERSTOCK. Tone of voice.

SYBIL. I suppose over the years they get to know, don't they, which kind of voice is the one that's most successful for the purpose, and gradually weed out the others.

MRS. CRABBE-HARMSWORTH. It's the expression too. On the face.

MISS HAVERGAL. On television.

SYBIL. Who was that newsreader . . . ?

CLARENCE. Yes.

SYBIL. During the flood disaster. We both commented.

CLARENCE. Yes. I know the one you mean.

MISS HAVERGAL. Some of them have a most off-putting demeanor.

SYBIL. This one did.

CLARENCE. Half smile.

SYBIL. Yes.

CLARENCE. As if he was trying his damnedest not to laugh.

MRS. CRABBE-HARMSWORTH. And that look on their faces as though it were really all rather jolly, don't you know.

SYBIL. Well, certainly no one would ever have imagined, would they, that it was one of the largest floods in history . . . wasn't it? . . . with goodness knows how many people drowned and untold damage to property as well to make things worse.

BAVERSTOCK. If they don't take it seriously, how can they expect the rest of us to? (Pause.)

VOICE (offstage). Heeeeeeeelp! Heeeeeeelp!

BAVERSTOCK. Not but what it's possible to get too concerned.

CLARENCE. Oh, yes.

BAVERSTOCK. So much time worrying about the problems of other people that in the end you've got no time left to deal with your own.

MRS. CRABBE-HARMSWORTH. It's not as if . . . when you do express concern . . . that it's ever reciprocated.

VOICE (offstage). Heeeeeeeelp! Heeeeeeelp!

BAVERSTOCK. Too busy mulling over their own troubles . . . like our friend out there. Get preoccupied with their situation to the exclusion of everything else.

MRS. CRABBE-HARMSWORTH. Talking about

drowning, I wonder if one dare venture on deck.

MISS HAVERGAL. Shall I . . . ?

MRS. CRABBE-HARMSWORTH. No. I think better not. The less notice one takes the better. He's only trying to draw attention to himself. The best thing is to ignore it. If it becomes too nerve-racking, we shall have to come below again.

SYBIL (to CLARENCE). Shall we be intrepid?

CLARENCE. Yes, I suppose there's no point in remaining cloistered down here for the rest of the day.

BAVERSTOCK. Yes. I think I'll join you. (They all begin to get up and leave.)

(NOTE: Under the guise of dispersing and going up on deck, they re-group for Scene Three, using the tail-end of the shipboard conversation as a bridge from one to the other.)

SYBIL. One can only hope that some action's being taken somewhere to get things moving.

MRS. CRABBE-HARMSWORTH. If he must drown, why can't he be given some form of inducement for getting it over and done with. In the form of compensation or something.

SYBIL. That would be too obvious.

CLARENCE. Red tape and bureaucracy.

BAVERSTOCK. One of the good things to be said for Hilter. At least he got things done. Committees for this, committees for that. Delays here, delays there.

CLARENCE. Insufferable.

(PUTNEY enters, passing the other way.)

PUTNEY. Seems to be in a bad way.

BAVERSTOCK. Yes.

PUTNEY. Watching it downstairs on the closed circuit television. Brings it home to you when you see it on the box.

SYBIL. One can only hope that a more live-wire body is in charge of that particular situation.

BLACKOUT

Scene 3

AS LIGHTS come up on Committee Room, we see sitting: MR. BURBAGE (played by Mr. Williams) as CHAIRMAN: MRS. CARTHAGE (played by Miss Stewart); MR. CLAPTON (played by Mr. Vernon); MISS RUGG (played by Sybil). MRS. WHITBRACE sits watching as they consider her case. Committee all have copies of Memorandum in front of them.

CHAIRMAN. . . . and which has been passed to us a possibly deserving cause.

MRS. CARTHAGE. Submitted (Checks date.) some few weeks ago . . .

MISS RUGG. It was passed to us too late to be included on last month's agenda.

CHAIRMAN. Rather unfortunate in view of the delay already experienced, but one of those things that happen, through no one's fault. Mrs. Whitbrace has received, I think I'm right in saying, a letter of apology.

MISS RUGG (with letter; reading). "Dear Mrs. Whitbrace: First of all may I apologize most sincerely for the delay in acknowledging your letter of application in respect to your husband's rescue . . . (Skims down page.) . . . rather snowed under, as you probably realize, with all the various preparations in connection with World National Help-You-Out Year Week . . . stateless citizen in international waters without proper papers . . . difficulties, as you can imagine . . . successful conclusion nevertheless . . . all good wishes for a happy outcome. . . . Yours etc." (They beam as one man at

MRS. WHITBRACE by way of identifying with this sentiment, then drift back one by one to business. MRS. CARTHAGE makes a general comment.)

MRS. CARTHAGE. This is not, of course, the first time, is it, that Mrs. Whitbrace has made application for rescue to one authority or another. I see she made application in 1959 . . .

MRS. WHITBRACE. Ah, yes, well, you see . . .

MRS. CARTHAGE. . . . when he got carried out beyond his depth at Clacton.

MRS. WHITBRACE. I can explain that . . .

MRS. CARTHAGE. Not to mention the Bristol Channel in July 1962.

CLAPTON. And the Firth of Forth a few months after that.

MRS. WHITBRACE. It all started when he fell off a breakwater at Dungeness, you see . . .

MRS. CARTHAGE. I think we should make very clear to Mrs. Whitbrace, that rescue . . . if it were to be eventually forthcoming . . . must not be taken as giving carte blanche the moment he's out of the water to go straight back and fall into the Panama Canal . . . or some other such stretch of water.

CHAIRMAN. Yes.

MRS. CARTHAGE (to MRS. WHITBRACE). In the past, when rescue has come too soon and too easily, it has all too often been interpreted as giving a kind of official sanction to the act of falling overboard . . .

MRS. WHITBRACE. Oh, no. He wouldn't take advantage. He's not like that at all.

CHAIRMAN. You see, the problem from our point of view, Mrs. . . . (Checks name.) . . . Whitbrace . . . as you can, I'm sure, imagine . . . is that we are disposing here of public money, and . . . with this kind of recent history . . . we have to ask ourselves what guarantee there is that we shouldn't simply be wasting our time.

MRS. WHITBRACE. I do think this last one's been a lesson to him, I really do.

CHAIRMAN. Yes. There are, as you probably know, certain difficulties . . . the solving of which is largely out of our hands . . . but there's no reason at all why nevertheless the ground shouldn't be cleared, so that the moment we get the green light we can go full steam ahead and refer the thing forward for more or less immediate action. There is, as you probably know, in the normal course of events, a waiting list procedure, but this, in view of the special circumstances, we might be able to find a way of side-stepping.

MRS. WHITBRACE. Oh, well, thank you very much. It's every time he sees a stretch of salt water, you see. He can't resist it. I'm sure he'd be willing to undergo treatment once he was rescued.

CHAIRMAN. One thing which I have been asked to put to you . . . I think, Mr. Clapton . . .

CLAPTON. Yes. It occurs to me to ask you, Mrs. . . . (Checks name.) . . . Whitbrace . . . in view of the fact that urgency seems to be something of a factor . . . whether it has crossed your mind to look into the possibility at all of having him rescued privately.

MRS. WHITBRACE. Well . . .

MISS RUGG. Or of taking out insurance against the possibility of his falling overboard again at some time, which would then make private rescue available to you should you want it.

MRS. WHITBRACE. Yes, well, I know one should look ahead . . .

CLAPTON. Because, as you probably know, it is

occasionally possible, in the private sector, to fit someone in a shade more quickly than one might otherwise be able to.

CHAIRMAN. Without prejudice of course, in any way, to the interests of others in equal need of rescue . . .

CLAPTON. Quite. And who will have to wait their turn a little longer as a result.

MRS. WHITBRACE. Yes, I'd like to, but . . . the fees, you see . . . which is really why I wanted it done, if possible, under the welfare.

CHAIRMAN. Yes. Quite. It was just a thought.

MRS. CARTHAGE. Before we leave the question of rescue . . . I see that Mrs. . . . (Turns memorandum over for name.) Whitbrace . . . has expressed a preference for having the rescue carried out if possible locally, as soon as the go-ahead comes through. Is that feasible?

CHAIRMAN. Assuming they have their own facilities. They presumably know more about the local situation than anyone.

CLAPTON. When we say locally . . .

CHAIRMAN. Bay of Naples, isn't it? To all intents and purposes.

MRS. CARTHAGE. On the other hand . . . do you really want the attentions of complete strangers in a situation like that? I should have thought, if you were drowning, you'd want to have dealings so far as possible with people who know something about you.

CLAPTON. Preferably who've rescued you before.

CHAIRMAN. Own kith and kin.

MRS. WHITBRACE. Well . . . ideally he would . . . but it's his life jacket, you see . . . it's getting waterlogged.

MISS RUGG. Besides which, standards are not all they might be in some of these places. One's had experiences before.

CHAIRMAN. True.

CLAPTON. We're not all that far from the coast of Sicily, are we?

MRS. CARTHAGE. Sicily?

CLAPTON. Yes. One or two rumors as to who runs the lifeboat service in that part of the world.

MRS. CARTHAGE. Mafia.

CHAIRMAN. Ah.

MISS RUGG. We don't want to find ourselves running too closely in harness with that kind of body.

CHAIRMAN. No.

MISS RUGG. Some rough diamonds, to say the least.

MRS. CARTHAGE. All too ready to resort to the harpoon for the sake of a quick rescue, if past experience is any guide.

CLAPTON. They're not as kid glove in their methods as one would like.

MRS. WHITBRACE. Actually, I think he'd almost rather . . .

MISS RUGG. See someone struggling in the water . . . they'd drop a depth charge as soon as look at him.

CHAIRMAN. Yes.

MISS RUGG. In certain moods.

CLAPTON. Blow you clean out of the water and shoot you down like a pheasant.

CHAIRMAN. Yes. I think we've got to accept that as far as rescue is concerned, the ball is fairly firmly in our court.

MRS. CARTHAGE. In view of which, it might be useful to ask Mrs. Whitbrace to be drawing up, if she can, during the next week or two, some sort of description of her husband for identification purposes at the time of rescue . . . so that they can have some idea what kind of a person it is that they're looking for.

CHAIRMAN (to MRS. WHITBRACE). Is that?

MRS. WHITBRACE. Yes . . . well, he's a tall man with glasses and a slight stoop.

CHAIRMAN. Yes . . .

MRS. WHITBRACE. He's very easy to recognize. In fact, I've got a photograph . . . (Hands it to CHAIRMAN. It is passed around and back to MRS. WHITBRACE.) It's his married sister in Dumfries, but they're identical to look at.

CHAIRMAN. Good. So if you could get all that down on paper for us, I think we can turn to more immediate practicalities . . . which boils down to what use Mr. . . . Whitbrace is making . . . in the meantime . . . of his time in the water. And whether he could in any way be spending it more profitably.

MRS. WHITBRACE. Well . . .

CHAIRMAN. Because . . . just bobbing about on the surface day after day . . . it's hardly a very rewarding or constructive way, is it, of spending one's time . . .

MRS. WHITBRACE. Well, no, I suppose not, but . . .

MRS. CARTHAGE. Perhaps Mrs. Whitbrace could give us some idea of the sort of thing that he *has* been occupying himself with?

CHAIRMAN. What has he been up to?

MRS. WHITBRACE. Up to?

CLAPTON. I don't think Mr. Burbage was suggesting another woman or anything, Mrs. Whitbrace. We were just wondering how he's been occupying his time for the six weeks or so that he's been in the water.

MRS. WHITBRACE. Oh.

MRS. CARTHAGE. Has he made any efforts to help himself at all? By trying to swim ashore, for instance?

MRS. WHITBRACE. He can't swim, you see. That's

part of the trouble.

MISS RUGG. Has he made a token gesture?

MRS. CARTHAGE. One can nearly always do something to propel oneself along, if only by flapping one's wrists about.

MRS. WHITBRACE. I think his mind's more taken up with trying to keep afloat, really.

CHAIRMAN. Yes.

MRS. WHITBRACE. It's every time he goes under, you see. It's all he can do to breathe.

MRS. CARTHAGE. One knows it isn't ideal conditions, but I should have thought if ever there were a heaven-sent opportunity to learn a second trade . . .

CHAIRMAN. Yes.

MRS. CARTHAGE. Such as bricklaying.

CHAIRMAN. Or accountancy.

MRS. CARTHAGE. I don't know what he is in civilian life . . .

MRS. WHITBRACE. He's a bookmaker's runner.

MRS. CARTHAGE. If only to have something to fall back on when eventually he sets foot on dry land again, if he ever does, and finds bookmaking a dead letter.

MRS. WHITBRACE. I think it was more rescue, really . . .

MRS. CARTHAGE. Or basketmaking. It's a chance to better himself that a lot of people would jump at, and it's one that might never come again.

CLAPTON. Weaving.

MRS. CARTHAGE. They can all be done by correspondence.

CHAIRMAN. Perhaps, Miss Rugg . . .

MISS RUGG. Yes. I was going to add bookbinding and raffia-work.

CLAPTON. Bearing in mind, that if he takes <u>too</u> much on, of course, he's going to have precious little time to call for help.

CHAIRMAN. A question of organizing his day properly . . .

MRS. CARTHAGE. I'm more inclined to think that . . . all work and no play . . . we should think in terms of cultural activities as well, that give him something to live for other than just material things.

CLAPTON. The whole man.

MRS. CARTHAGE. I don't know what sort of leisure pursuits he normally follows . . .

CHAIRMAN. Perhaps, Mrs. Whitbrace . . .

MRS. WHITBRACE. Well . . .

CLAPTON. Art . . . music . . . literature . . . ?

MRS. WHITBRACE. Well, most of the time . . .

MRS. CARTHAGE. You see, my own feeling here is that we could do worse than think in terms of a small piano.

CLAPTON. Take his mind off things with an occasional Brandenburg Concerto. Not a bad thought.

MRS. CARTHAGE. It has always been part of Help-You-Out Year Week policy to give encouragement wherever possible to the arts, and this would seem to be a golden opportunity.

CHAIRMAN. One obviously would want to lend a more than sympathetic ear to anything of that nature that could be shown to be of definite cultural value . . . on the other hand, once drowning comes to be seen as a short cut to a musical instrument . . .

MRS. CARTHAGE. There's the possibility that he'll make use of it simply to keep afloat on . . . but anything, after all, can be abused. And I think one should give him the benefit of the doubt.

CLAPTON. The ultimate aim, of course, being rescue.

MISS RUGG. Oh, yes.

CLAPTON. I don't think one wants to lose sight of that.

CHAIRMAN. Oh, no. These are purely interim measures.

MISS RUGG. And will be throughout.

CHAIRMAN. In the meantime . . . if we can set Mrs. Whitbrace's mind at rest . . . with regard to action being taken elsewhere . . .

(The CHAIRMAN looks around in an upstage direction, where without losing the committee room scene, lights go up on a SOLICITOR /played by Mr. Putney/ talking with measured langor on the telephone.)

SOLICITOR. . . . Yes. . . . Yes. . . . (Glances at wall map.) Well, he's more or less plumb in the middle of one of the main shipping lanes, so . . . Yes. . . . Yes. . . . If they have to change course to avoid him, obviously there's no question that it involves them in a measure of inconvenience, but as I read the situation at this stage, it falls a long way short of constituting a nuisance within the meaning of the Act . . . Yes. . . . Yes. . . . (Fumbles among papers on desk.) Yes, I've got the papers here in front of me. . . . Feelings are bound to run a bit high in a situation like that and if it's keeping them awake at night of course they've obviously got a certain amount of justice on their side - on the other hand, if a drowning man can't call for help, who on earth can? . . . Yes. . . . (From legal document; reading.) ". . . bring to your attention . . . drownee's signature to an undertaking countersigned by you as his legal representative . . . to refrain from shouts of 'Help!' during the hours of darkness and at such other times . . . " It's a fairly standard document and they're perfectly within their rights in making representations but . . . Well, yes. She's with the Committee now. . . . But to invite a wife to knock her husband unconscious with a mallet, even for his own and other people's good, could create a dangerous precedent. . . . It is - quite iniquitous. . . . One gathers the last straw was when they were asked to have a whip around for throat lozenges for him. . . . (Lights begin to fade as SOLICITOR reads from document again.) ". . . grace and favor allowance of up to but not exceeding a total of ten seconds in every hour . . . to the annoyance of bona fide passengers . . ."

(The lights fade down on the SOLICITOR and our attention is turned back to the Committee Room.)

CHAIRMAN. Yes. I don't think any of that need concern us, and in fact . . . (To MRS. WHITBRACE.) I think we can . . .

MRS. WHITBRACE (getting up). Well, thank you very much. I'm ever so grateful.

MISS RUGG (to CHAIRMAN). Rescue Card.

CHAIRMAN. Ah. (To MRS. WHITBRACE.) Before you go. Miss Rugg wants to have a word about . . .

MISS RUGG. Mr. Whitbrace's Rescue Card.

MRS. WHITBRACE. Oh . . .

MISS RUGG. If he could have it on him at the moment of rescue fully stamped up . . .

CHAIRMAN. Otherwise it's another forty-eight hours in the water and a lot of fuss and bother all around while we chase it up.

MISS RUGG. He can claim relief on the postage by filling in the appropriate form and sending it in together with a stamped addressed envelope.

MRS. WHITBRACE. Thank you very much. I'm sure if he'd thought it was going to create so much trouble, he'd have thought twice about falling in.

CHAIRMAN. Let's hope that in six months' time the situation will be looking a whole lot brighter than it does at present. (Committee breaks up and begins to disperse, speaking to MRS. WHITBRACE in turn.)

MISS RUGG. We do encourage people to find out in advance what the rescue position is, before committing themselves, especially outside home waters . . . but the important thing now is to try to keep his spirits up and prevent him getting too despondent.

MRS. CARTHAGE. And when he does eventually come home that he'll in all probability be dripping wet . . . so have a nice warm fire waiting for him and a plentiful supply of towels.

CLAPTON. Remember that if the worst comes to the worst, he can always drown, so it's not the end of the world.

MRS. WHITBRACE (going). Well, thank you very much. I'm ever so grateful.

CHAIRMAN. Not at all, Mrs. Whitbrace. It's what we're here for.

(As the committee regroups for the next scene, MRS. WHITBRACE is approached by a GIRL REPORTER /played by Miss Hughes/ along the upstage ramp.)

REPORTER. Mrs. Whitbrace? I'm from *Teenager*. What's it like to be the wife of someone who has been treading water now for upwards of fifteen weeks? Does it get you down at all?

MRS. WHITBRACE. Well . . . not to say down . . . I

. . . I mean, you get used to it.

REPORTER. It hasn't made any appreciable difference to you?

MRS. WHITBRACE. Not really.

REPORTER. In fact, for all the effect it's had on you, you feel you might just as well be Florence Nightingale's married sister . . . is that what you're really trying to tell me?

MRS. WHITBRACE. Well . . . you come to accept it, don't you?

REPORTER. Yes. I notice that . . . (Refers to notes.) Keats' well known reference to the season of mists and mellow fruitfulness in his Ode to Autumn . . . did this have any appreciable influence, do you think, on Mr. Whitbrace's decision to fall overboard in the spring at all?

MRS. WHITBRACE. I don't think so. If it did, he never mentioned it.

REPORTER. I see. And what . . . if the opportunity presented itself . . . would be his attitude to falling overboard again at some time. Would he do it in the same way, or would he try it slightly differently?

MRS. WHITBRACE. We've never properly discussed it. He's always done it in the same way in the past.

REPORTER. By . . .

MRS. WHITBRACE. Well, just . . . you know . . .

REPORTER. Toppling . . .

MRS. WHITBRACE. Yes. Head first.

REPORTER. Thank you very much, Mrs. Whitbrace. (REPORTER and MRS. WHITBRACE go off.)

BLACKOUT

Scene 4

AS LIGHTS come up on the ship's lounge, we see sitting: CLARENCE and SYBIL, MRS. CRABBE-HARMSWORTH and MISS HAVERGAL and BAVERSTOCK.

CLARENCE. At least his lordship out there seems to have quietened down a bit.

MRS. CRABBE-HARMSWORTH. It might almost be safe to have the porthole open.

SYBIL. Dare we risk it, do you think?

BAVERSTOCK. It seemed all clear during dinner. (Pause.)

MISS HAVERGAL. Shall I . . . ? (No one answers and she goes to the porthole and opens it. She stands for a moment looking out, and then goes back to her chair.) They're just lowering it to him now. With the aid of floodlights. (Pause.)

SYBIL. Why he needs a piano at all, let alone a baby grand.

MRS. CRABBE-HARMSWORTH. Well, quite.

BAVERSTOCK. Sitting target for the first plausible rogue that comes along.

SYBIL. Of course he is.

BAVERSTOCK. Some less scrupulous gentleman from the Middle East with a smooth tongue and an eye to the main chance. Turns up with a suitcase full of reconditioned outboard motors, and in no time at all he's got two of them clamped to the keyboard and he's sighted going like the clappers through the Straits of Gibraltar en route for the West Indies. Ends up in the Bahamas - basking in the sun at public expense.

SYBIL. It's asking for it.

BAVERSTOCK. Hi-jacked on the way - ends up in Cuba. Whole thing escalates and before we know what's hit us there's Russia, America and China involved and we're sitting pretty with two dozen nuclear holocausts on our hands.

CLARENCE. It's a frightening thought.

BAVERSTOCK. While Johnny boy retires in luxury to Morocco, having made a small fortune out of the gullibility of the rest of us. (Pause. First two bars of Mendelssohn's Wedding March on the distant piano.)

MRS. CRABBE-HARMSWORTH. If he must have a musical instrument, I should have thought a flute would have been perfectly adequate.

SYBIL. And safer. (Pause. Same two bars again, then three bars, then silence.)

MISS HAVERGAL. While someone like Yehudi Menuhin . . .

SYBIL. Oh, well.

BAVERSTOCK. That's a different matter. (Pause.) You have to be one of the privileged. Floundering about in the Mediterranean with one sock on and one sock off, if you want a grand piano in this day and age. Being a world-famous musician doesn't qualify. If you're no one more important than Yehudi Menuhin, you make do as best you can.

SYBIL. Quite.

BAVERSTOCK. Fend for yourself. Forgetting to fall overboard off a banana boat at an early age. That's where Yehudi Menuhin made his mistake. Had the good sense to fall off the pier at Clacton when he was first starting out, and you wouldn't be able to see him now for harpsichords. (Pause.) One of the top keyboard instrumentalists of all time by now. Up there on the concert platforms of the world with Primo Carnera and

Helena Rubinstein. (Pause.) Instead of which he has to make do with a violin. (Pause.)

CLARENCE. Pretty sad commentary.

BAVERSTOCK. It is.

CLARENCE. On the sort of world we live in. (Sound of distant piano being tuned. MISS HAVERGAL goes to the porthole and looks out.)

MISS HAVERGAL. They've just lowered a piano-tuner to him. (Resigned silence.)

MRS. CRABBE-HARMSWORTH. Better than "Help Help Help" all the time, I suppose.

SYBIL. That really was becoming insufferable.

MISS HAVERGAL. Shall I . . . ?

MRS. CRABBE-HARMSWORTH. Yes, I think you'd better, Elspeth. (MISS HAVERGAL closes porthole.)

BLACKOUT

Scene 5

LIGHTS come up on the Cerebral House. We see a modern office. A large wall map is covered with small red flags, and a wall chart in the form of a giant calendar is labeled "Albert Whitbrace Scheme." Days are marked off on it to signify how long he has been in the water. Visible are the following posters:

World National Help-You-Out Year Week Special Appeals Campaign: much has been done - much remains to be done. Will you help?

No man need be an island!

Do you know someone in trouble? Help us to help him help himself during World National Help-You-Out Year Week! And win a free trip for two to the Bay of Naples!

Buy it now! "Cries for help through the ages."

The telephone rings. MISS LINTHROPP (played by Miss Hughes), as secretary to PUTNEY, answers it. MRS. CLACTON (played by Sybil) is typing at another desk.

MISS LINTHROPP. Cerebral House. World National Help-You-Out Year Week Special Appeals Campaign Special Advisory Service. May I help you? . . . Yes. . . . Yes. . . . (MRS. CLACTON'S telephone rings.)

MRS. CLACTON (into telephone). Cerebral House. World National Help-You-Out Year Week Special

Appeals Campaign Central Advisory Service. May I help you? . . . Not at all. (She hangs up telephone. MISS LINTHROPP goes past MRS. CLACTON on her way out, having laid her telephone receiver on her desk.) Two teas, one without sugar, and a plate of biscuits. I ask you! (MRS. CLACTON resumes her typing.)

MISS LINTHROPP. It's a wrong number. They think we're the Feedwell Cafe or something. We're always getting them. (Telephone rings again.)

MRS. CLACTON. Oh, no. (MISS LINTHROPP exits as she picks up telephone; into telephone.) Cerebral House. World National Help-You-Out Year Week Special Appeals Campaign Central Advisory Service. May I help you? . . . Yes. . . . Well, it's not generally known, Mrs. Bleachbaker, that an errant kiteholder, who has abandoned his kite after persuading an innocent and all too good-natured passerby to take hold of it for a few moments - in this case your husband - in order, ostensibly, to nip off around the corner to buy his aunt a pair of bedsocks at Derry and Toms, can be compelled through the courts to return and take custody of his own kite - though first, of course, he must be found, and all too often, I'm afraid, we find when we come to look for him that he has departed hotfoot for the Argentine, where one's hope of catching up with him and bringing him to book is minimal. . . . On where? On an ice-floe in Alaska. I see. In that case I think we ought to consider forming a Society of Friends of Harry Bleachbaker, who will keep in touch and perhaps - in conjunction with Heinz or one of the other big manufacturers - send him out a plate of hot spaghetti once a fortnight or so. Anyway, leave it to me,

Mrs. Bleachbaker, and we'll look into the possibilities and let you know. . . . Not at all. It's what we're here for. . . . Good-bye, Mrs. Bleachbaker. (She hangs up the telephone and resumes her typing.)

(PUTNEY enters with MRS. WHITBRACE.)

MRS. WHITBRACE. It's his lifejacket, you see. It's getting waterlogged.

PUTNEY. It would be. After all this time. It's to be expected. Nothing to worry about there. The thing we're more interested in here is . . . (Finds telephone off cradle on desk.) What's this?

(MISS LINTHROPP enters.)

MISS LINTHROPP. Oh, that's the Daily Express Action Line people, Mr. Putney. They'd like you to ring them about a Mr. Wethershed.

PUTNEY. Who?

MISS LINTHROPP. He's the one who's stuck on a ledge in the Himalayas. He's been there since last Thanksgiving Day, and he's pestering them about what can they do as he's feeling the cold at night.

PUTNEY. Right.

MISS LINTHROPP. We've already arranged for him to be allowed access by proxy to a hot cocoa vending machine, but . . . (PUTNEY picks up telephone.)

PUTNEY (to MISS LINTHROPP as she exits). Yes. (Into telephone.) Putney here. Mr. Wethershed . . . Yes, that's right. . . . Well, we've been on to W.V.S. International about that, and they've very generously stepped in and arranged with their people on the spot in Nepal to have it re-heated on arrival, so that's no problem, but we're still in touch with Pan Am about using one of their scheduled flights to . . . In cardboard cups, yes. . . . Would you? . . . Well, there's always the possibility we might get a small news item out of it and a picture. One of their stewardesses carrying it on to the aircraft. . . . Yes. . . . Well, it's not the kind of thing that's going to do their image any harm, put it that way. . . . And then for the last few thousand feet by sherpa. . . . Not at all. Thank you. (He hangs up telephone, and turns to MRS. WHITBRACE:) Now. Yes. Mr. Albert Whitbrace. . . .

MRS. WHITBRACE. We were talking about his life-jacket.

PUTNEY. His what?

MRS. WHITBRACE. Well . . . his . . . his Mae West. It's getting a bit . . .

PUTNEY. Waterlogged. Yes. That's an occupational hazard so far as drowning is concerned, I'm afraid. It's something he'll have to learn to live with . . . or drown with, I suppose I should say . . . because, as you probably know . . . (He crosses to a huge wall map covered with red flags. MR. WHITBRACE'S position in the mediterranean is marked by a large gold star.) we intend, as we expand, to make Mr. Whitbrace very much the focus of our activities. We're counting on his stay in the water being reasonably prolonged, being so, I think we can all . . . including you and your husband . . . expect to benefit quite materially, as time goes on, from the various quite exciting schemes we've got in the pipeline.

MRS. WHITBRACE. Well . . . the thing was . . .

really . . .

PUTNEY. Such as, amongst other things, the piano . . . which I believe he's now fully conversant with the use of and which, as you know, was supplied to him by courtesy of Musical Supply Enterprises on condition the name Honegger Pianos was illuminated at night in such a way as to be visible to aircraft at a height of fifteen thousand feet.

MRS. WHITBRACE. Well . . . about the piano . . .

PUTNEY. And of course, if we could get some press and television coverage of him actually playing the instrument, it would help us immeasurably with public relations.

MRS. WHITBRACE. Yes, he does realize that, but . . .

PUTNEY. Which is what the various sponsors, such as Musical Supply Enterprises, would naturally look for . . . so that they can feel that to have taken part in the project on humanitarian grounds in the generous and altruistic way we hope they will be doing, is not a complete waste of time and money for them.

(MISS LINTHROPP enters.)

MISS LINTHROPP. The Prime Minister's Press Representative on the line, Mr. Putney. . . . Can we arrange at all for Mrs. Whitbrace to be at Ten Downing Street this afternoon, so that the Prime Minister can be photographed speaking sympathetically to her and pledging his full backing and personal intervention at top level should it become necessary or advisable.

PUTNEY. Good.

MRS. CLACTON. My word. You've arrived.

MRS. WHITBRACE. Have I?

PUTNEY. Good heavens, yes. No Prime Minister bothers himself with this kind of thing unless you look like becoming headline material.

MRS. WHITBRACE. Oh.

PUTNEY. So congratulations. You'll need to dress up a little bit, but there'll be advice available on that, and in the meantime . . . yes . . . the piano . . .

MRS. WHITBRACE. Well, it's his sostenuto pedal, you see.

PUTNEY. What's wrong with his sostenuto pedal?

MRS. WHITBRACE. He can't get a proper purchase on it. He really needs a piano stool. Only with the piano bobbing about in the water . . . and in a high sea . . . he keeps missing it with his foot.

PUTNEY. Yes.

MRS. WHITBRACE. And he's only got his socks on, so that when he does find it, he as often as not stubs his toe on it. Especially as it's a bit stiff. And it means he can't get the best out of the keyboard.

PUTNEY. Yes . . . well, this looks like something for the piano engineer when he comes in. (Telephone rings. PUTNEY picks it up; into telephone:) Yes? . . . Right. (He hangs up telephone and gets up. To MRS. WHITBRACE:) Archbishop of Canterbury.

(PUTNEY exits as MISS LINTHROPP comes in with piano ENGINEER /played by Mr. Vernon/.)

MISS LINTHROPP. Over here. She's complaining about the piano. He seems to be having trouble with it.

ENGINEER. What's the problem?

MRS. WHITBRACE. Well . . . it's not really working

as it should be. They seemed to think it was his fault.

ENGINEER. Let's take a common-sense view of this, shall we? He was trying to get classical music out of it, and it wasn't ever built for that. In fact it isn't even in the proper sense an amphibious piano in the first place. It had to be adapted.

MISS LINTHROPP. Ah.

ENGINEER. You can't go pounding away like he was . . . trying to get Berlioz' "Dance of the Bumble-bees" out of a tarted-up pub piano that was never intended for use on the high seas in the first place. Reasonable use, yes. But that, quite frankly, is ridiculous.

MISS LINTHROPP. Something about his sostenuto pedal.

ENGINEER. There's nothing wrong with his sostenuto pedal. The sostenuto pedal's the one thing that's working perfectly. It's been put through every test known to man . . . in water and out of it . . .

MISS LINTHROPP. He can't seem to get at it or something, with his foot.

MRS. WHITBRACE. He's wearing socks, you see.

ENGINEER. Socks or snowshoes . . . it makes no difference. It's not the fault of the sostenuto pedal if his legs are sawn off at the knees.

MISS LINTHROPP. Well . . .

ENGINEER. American organ, you'd have the same problem.

MISS LINTHROPP. Could it be put higher up, perhaps?

ENGINEER. Feasible. But . . . yes - all right. We can but try. (He exits.)

MISS LINTHROPP. I don't know what his attitude would be . . . once we can get the bugs ironed out . . . to the idea of giving the odd recital . . .

MRS. WHITBRACE. Well . . .

MISS LINTHROPP. The Albert Whitbrace Half-hour.

MRS. WHITBRACE. I'm not sure whether he's up to that standard.

MISS LINTHROPP. Regale the world with a bit of Carmen's *Bizet* . . . which we could pick up live by satellite and send out on simultaneous transmission to such of the member countries as might be interested in receiving it . . .

(MISS LINTHROPP breaks off and goes out, as PUTNEY comes back in with the ARCHBISHOP [played by Mr. Williams].)

PUTNEY (in the middle of a conversation with the ARCHBISHOP). The point being that there's a very genuine public concern beginning to build up at grass roots level. . . .

ARCHBISHOP. And this is where one could see the Church entering in and playing its part, under God, in broadening out the whole basis of our compassion . . . to include not just ourselves and those like-minded with us, but all those nations of the world which are torn by conflict and rent by strife, and which is our perhaps too narrow concern with the purely material needs of . . . of our friend in the water . . . we may be in danger of losing sight.

PUTNEY. Well, yes, this was . . .

ARCHBISHOP. Nothing would be more tragic than that in our very legitimate concern for his day-to-day comforts, he should become with the very best of intentions no more than a convenient object on which to exercise all manner of no doubt well-thought-out schemes for his physical betterment totally without regard for those greater spiritual needs and . . . and opportunities made possible through his brief . . . his brief sojourn in the . . . the Sargasso Sea.

PUTNEY. The Mediterranean. . . .
ARCHBISHOP. The Mediterranean Sea.
PUTNEY. Yes . . . well, in that respect, we were wondering . . .

(MISS LINTHROPP enters with grave face and a note, which PUTNEY reads with stunned incredulity and dismay as the ARCHBISHOP continues.)

ARCHBISHOP. So often do we find that those things which we may feel at first disposed to look upon, in mere human terms, as evils, are in God's hands the means whereby good may come . . . and that something which to the eye of reason may have seemed, all those many months ago, to have been no more than a simple untoward mishap to one of the least of God's children, will in His infinite wisdom and mercy become the occasion of something far greater . . .
PUTNEY (to MISS LINTHROPP). When did this come?
MISS LINTHROPP. Over the teleprinter just now.
ARCHBISHOP. . . . the germ, perhaps, of some great new initiative which will bring the nations of the world together in a common purpose of prayer and sympathy . . . a movement which will embrace both Russia and China in a spiritual rebirth such as we have not known since earliest palaeolithic times . . .
PUTNEY. We shall need your prayers, Archbishop.
MISS LINTHROPP. Everything going swimmingly for him, and then . . . ! (PUTNEY hands message to ARCHBISHOP, as he goes out with MRS. CLACTON and MISS LINTHROPP.)
ARCHBISHOP (reading message). ". . . inevitably overshadowed by a piece of news which many of you must have read with deep dismay in your papers at breakfast this morning . . ."

(MRS. WHITBRACE, sensing disaster, is trying to read the message over his shoulder.)

ARCHBISHOP. Official go-ahead on rescue! (MRS. WHITBRACE and ARCHBISHOP look at each other in frozen horror.)

BLACKOUT

Scene 6

AS LIGHTS come up we see CABINET MINISTER (played by Mr. Williams) and SENIOR CIVIL SERVANT (played by Mr. Vernon) in the Cabinet Room.)

MINISTER. Caught with our trousers down.

SENIOR. We could hardly have been expected to foresee rescue coming up.

MINISTER. The Albert Whitbrace Scheme . . . the Albert Whitbrace Research Fellowship . . .

SENIOR. The Albert Whitbrace Rehabilitation Centre at Hemel Hempstead.

MINISTER. Every single one a dead duck.

SENIOR. They certainly look like becoming unfulfilled dreams.

MINISTER. Poor old Reggie. He was looking to those, bless him, for his K.

SENIOR. He's not the only one who'll feel it.

MINISTER. Oh, no. It's going to have its repercussions everywhere.

SENIOR (reading telegram). ". . . without consultation and totally without regard for the human issues involved . . . thousands of lower paid workers in the Piano Distribution and Allied Trades . . . no one opposed to rescue at the right time and in the right place . . . fight it tooth and nail every inch of the way . . . sincerely hope we shall see reason prevail in this matter . . . courage and vision to think again. Vic Feather."

MINISTER. We shall be getting a good few more like that before the day's out.

SENIOR (with several telegrams). In fact there

seems to be a very genuine groundswell of public opinion beginning to build up. (Reading one of the telegrams.) The Hands Off Albert Whitbrace Interim Emergency Committee . . . just one word . . . "Pigs!"

MINISTER (reading another telegram). "A Protest Float-In at Camberwell Baths. See you there, buster!" (We hear a shouting, chanting crowd outside window, saying things like: "Hands Off Albert Whitbrace!" MINISTER crosses to window and closes it, shutting out sound.) We're in a constitutionally cleft stick. Precious little we can do within the law, and on the other hand if we sit back and do nothing . . . if we simply let things take their course and look helplessly on while he's being willy-nilly rescued . . . and without lifting a finger to prevent it . . . we shall have the Civil Liberties people down on us like a ton of bricks, breathing fire and brimstone and heaven knows what else.

(They freeze as MRS. WHITBRACE enters and crosses with GIRL REPORTER.)

MRS. WHITBRACE. Well, yes, it is. A complete surprise.

REPORTER. It must be something of a bodyblow for you, coming when everything was going so well for you.

MRS. WHITBRACE. It is. Only last week he was due to be made honorary freeman in his absence of the Bristol Channel . . . which would have been quite a feather for him, because they were very nasty to him when he fell in there nine years ago and this would have been . . .

REPORTER. Poetic justice.

MRS. WHITBRACE. Well, yes . . . and now, of

course, with this coming up it's all in the melting pot again.

REPORTER. Do you intend to fight back at all so far as rescue is concerned?

MRS. WHITBRACE. Well, yes, we're hoping to organize a protest meeting.

REPORTER. How is your husband taking it, Mrs. Whitbrace, on the whole? Is he fairly philosophical about it? After all, you have <u>had</u> things going your way, haven't you, until <u>now</u>?

MRS. WHITBRACE. I think he's more or less resigned. He's always been fatalistic, you see. And we both had a premonition.

REPORTER. It's just the way the cookie crumbles, in other words.

MRS. WHITBRACE. Well, sort of, yes.

(MRS. WHITBRACE and REPORTER go off as MINISTER and SENIOR CIVIL SERVANT unfreeze.)

SENIOR. Were he in Scotland, of course . . .

MINISTER. In where?

SENIOR. Or had exercised the option, which he undoubtedly had, to withhold his consent in writing within the period of grace allotted, there's no power on earth could have done anything about it.

MINISTER. What's Scotland got to do with it?

SENIOR. The situation could well be very different . . .

MINISTER. Could it?

SENIOR. There's a whole untapped field of Scottish law which . . . with all that that could mean in terms of continuing litigation . . . could well carry into 1979 or even beyond that into 1984.

MINISTER. That would seem . . .

SENIOR. We have in fact looked into it.

MINISTER. One flaw . . . or what seems on the

face of it to be a flaw . . . the Mediterranean is not . . . I think I'm right in saying . . . in Scotland.

SENIOR. Ah. That, in law, need not be an obstacle.

(Lights go up on a brilliant but lofty YOUNG LAWYER expounding a thesis at a huge wall-map of Europe.)

LAWYER. It would be enough to show that it is in what . . . for the present purposes . . . can be deemed to be Scotland, and here we might usefully explore the possibility that Scotland . . . as we know it . . . may not always have occupied the precise position north of the border that it is commonly thought of as occupying today. We are assisted here by the known fact that the general configuration of the earth's surface, such as it is, was not arrived at overnight. It is the end product of a not unlengthy process involving widespread upheaval over a period of several millennia, during the course of which things were in a considerable state of flux . . . and it should not be difficult to demonstrate as a prior possibility that . . . (Points to map.) Scotland . . . or what was subsequently to become known as Scotland . . . might, in one of the remoter periods of geological time, have occupied, however fleetingly, and prior to making its journey northwards to the position on the map that it has occupied ever since . . . the very spot in the Mediterranean in which the drowning man is at present ensconced. If so, there would be a strong prima facie case for a re-appraisal of the whole situation with a view to bringing the whole matter fairly and squarely within the jurisdiction of the Scottish courts, where a whole new area of possibilities opens up which could bid fair to delay rescue for some considerable time to come.

(Lights dim down on LAWYER and our attention is again focused on the SENIOR CIVIL SERVANT and the MINISTER.)

SENIOR. Sounds promising.
MINISTER. Yes - I think one could give voice to a tentative eureka there.
SENIOR. In fact, the more one thinks about it . . .
MINISTER. Yes. It throws a positively brilliant . . . (Glances in the direction of the LAWYER.) spanner into the works.
SENIOR. Enabling us . . . to carry on precisely as though nothing untoward had occurred, and allow things to take their course without too much disruption . . . and in fact do everything that can be done to allay public disquiet. . . .
SENIOR. Yes - that is in hand.

BLACKOUT

Scene 7

LIGHTS come up on the Ship's Lounge. We hear the opening bars of Beethoven's Fifth Piano Concerto. The piano chords are full of mistakes, but the full orchestral accompaniment is perfect. BAVERSTOCK, MRS. CRABBE-HARMSWORTH, MISS HAVERGAL, and CLARENCE are looking out through the porthole.

MISS HAVERGAL. It looks like the Leningrad Symphony Orchestra. What's meant by a Russian presence in the Mediterranean, I suppose.

BAVERSTOCK. Trying to get in there for the last hundred and fifty years. They've made it at last. (MISS HAVERGAL closes the porthole as they all sit down.)

MRS. CRABBE-HARMSWORTH. One would be happier if one could feel his spiritual needs were being given equal attention.

CLARENCE. There's talk of having him sympathized with, isn't there? Professionally.

MRS. CRABBE-HARMSWORTH. It's certainly something that ought to be thought about. There's nothing a person needs more, in that situation, than proper sympathy.

MISS HAVERGAL. Mrs. Treplatchly, perhaps.

CLARENCE. Isn't that the woman who . . . ?

MRS. CRABBE-HARMSWORTH. . . . who founded Universal Wellwishers.

CLARENCE. I thought so.

BAVERSTOCK. Legend.

MRS. CRABBE-HARMSWORTH. Oh, yes.

BAVERSTOCK. In the sympathizing world. One of the top names.

MRS. CRABBE-HARMSWORTH. She could make short work of that situation out there.

BAVERSTOCK. Oh, yes. She could sympathize with someone like that blindfolded, and with one hand tied behind her back.

CLARENCE. And has done.

MRS. CRABBE-HARMSWORTH. Pity she isn't approached.

BAVERSTOCK. It would certainly relieve the wife. Someone to dwell sympathetically on his predicament for half an hour or so once a day, while she does her shopping.

CLARENCE. Godsend.

MRS. CRABBE-HARMSWORTH. In the meantime, we seem to be the object of attention ourselves.

(Television equipment is brought in.)

CLARENCE. "This Is Your Life," so someone was saying. Though why here, heaven only knows.

(MRS. TREPLATCHLY /played by Sybil/ enters in regal splendor and is settled into a thronelike chair for a deeply respectful interview.)

MISS HAVERGAL. Can it be . . . ?

MRS. CRABBE-HARMSWORTH. Surely not!

MISS HAVERGAL. It is. I'm sure it is. It's her!

(PUTNEY enters, takes up his position as interviewer, and launches straight in. Lights go down on the others and concentrate on PUTNEY and MRS. TREPLATCHLY, enabling Baverstock and Clarence to appear as DIRECTOR and PRODUCTION ASSISTANT when necessary.)

INTERVIEWER. Mrs. Treplatchly, as one of the world's most celebrated sympathizers, you have probably forgotten more about identifying with a fellow creature in distress than most of us ever knew . . . and as a result have been in constant demand wherever, as at this very moment, only a few hundred yards away, there have been those in need of help. Over the years you have sympathized with a host of people in all walks and stations of life, and royalty have been among your most enthusiastic and grateful clients. This perhaps is not surprising, since you come from a long line of distinguished sympathizers, one of whom . . . your maternal grandmother . . . was for a time chief mourner to the Hapsburg family, and was privileged in that capacity to shed tears at one time or another over most of the then crowned heads of Europe. You yourself have carried on the family tradition with triumphant success, as your appearance on this program testifies, and the question I would like to put to you, if I may, is "How much do you feel you owe to this long and distinguished family background?"

MRS. TREPLATCHLY. Oh, a very great deal. It's in one's blood, you see. You mentioned my grandmother, but of course there were so many of my relations who shared this family flair for sympathy . . . several of my aunts had it . . . one in particular . . . I remember her very well . . . had a most exceptional capacity for concern . . . so much so that it was remarked upon . . . and inevitably I suppose I must inherit some of it.

INTERVIEWER. You used the word "concern" . . . and this is a word which comes up whenever and wherever your name is spoken of . . . and especially concern for the less fortunate. How much, when it comes down to it, do most of us really care for those less fortunate than ourselves? And yet in the last analysis this is what being part of the human race is all about. You, Mrs. Treplatchly, care very much, and it was for this reason that back in 1923 you set up the organization then known as Universal Wellwishers . . . later to become Universal Prayer and Sympathy Services, Ltd. . . . and a household name wherever there are suffering people in need of comfort. For many years you were chronically understaffed at Universal Wellwishers, and in those days . . . even though as head of the organization you were busy with administrative work of all kinds . . . you were often prepared to neglect this . . . and, indeed, much of your own personal sympathizing, too . . . in order to come to the help of people who were relying on Universal Wellwishers not to let them down when some distant friend or loved one was in trouble. You are on record as saying that sympathy is a God-given gift. If so, it is a gift which you had in abundant measure . . . and to all who were able to pay your fees, you gave of it unstintingly.

MRS. TREPLATCHLY. How kind.

INTERVIEWER. Since those days you have had many triumphs, and amongst them was what I think is generally recognized as one of the finest pieces of virtuoso sympathizing ever recorded. . . . This was the occasion in 1970 when you showed such overwhelming concern for the plight of the Biafrans . . .

MRS. TREPLATCHLY. Oh, heavens!

INTERVIEWER. And they sent you a framed testimonial of their gratitude, which you have treasured ever since.

(Flash up framed testimonial.)

MRS. TREPLATCHLY. Indeed I have. I was most touched. (MRS. TREPLATCHLY wipes away a tear.)

INTERVIEWER. There was, of course, a precursor to this, earlier on in your chosen career, when on a celebrated occasion you gave promise of what was to lie ahead.

MRS. TREPLATCHLY. Oh, my goodness . . . ! Yes, I think I know what that must be.

INTERVIEWER. You had reached, you felt, a peak, and were ready for a greater challenge than any you had faced up to that time, and so, in 1953, you decided one day, quite out of the blue, to try and sympathize single-handed with the entire Chinese nation over the partial failure of their first Five Year Plan.

MRS. TREPLATCHLY. Yes . . . it was a foolhardy thing to do, looking back on it, but . . . if I could explain how it came about . . . I was, it's quite true, feeling restless at the time and looking around for new fields to conquer, and then, by the sheerest good luck, I saw an item of news in the paper about the Chinese and their First Five Year Plan. Well . . . obviously, it was far too good a chance to miss, and so . . . without saying a word to anyone . . . I gritted my teeth and said to myself: "Stephanie! this is your great opportunity! Seize it with both hands!" . . . and, of course, I did, and as luck would have it, I'm glad to say, managed to pull it off.

INTERVIEWER. Triumphantly . . . as the world now knows. And yet, at the time, a good many people advised you against it.

MRS. TREPLATCHLY. Oh, yes. All my friends were horrified. "Do you realize, Maude," they said, "just how many people there *are* in China? Do you realize what you're taking on?"

INTERVIEWER. This, of course, was at a time when the population of China was some four or five hundred million. . . .

MRS. TREPLATCHLY. Oh, yes. It was no picnic. And I gather it's a good deal more than that now, so it would be even less of a picnic if one were to try to do the same thing today. One thing, too, of course that helped was that at the time I happened by the purest chance to be suffering from a mild bout of jaundice . . . and . . .

INTERVIEWER. This must have been a great help in identifying.

MRS. TREPLATCHLY. It was. Oh, yes. And, of course, being able to bring it off did give me *the* most tremendous confidence. One felt that if one could do that, one could do anything and, in fact, one is very grateful *to* the People's Republic of China for giving one the opportunity. One got the most tremendous fillip out of it, as well as easing the burden a little bit, one hopes, for the Chinese people themselves at that rather critical time in their affairs.

INTERVIEWER. Would you do it again if the opportunity were to come your way?

MRS. TREPLATCHLY. Oh, yes! I should be absolutely thrilled! I should have to go behind a partition to limber up a little bit, because one gets rusty, but yes, if the opportunity came I'd leap at it, oh, most certainly!

INTERVIEWER. That, Mrs. Treplatchly, is very good news . . .

MRS. TREPLATCHLY. Oh, my goodness!

INTERVIEWER. . . . because it's my pleasure now to inform you that Mao Tse-tung and the entire Chinese people are on the other end of the line at this moment! . . .

MRS. TREPLATCHLY. Oh, no! (MRS. TREPLATCHLY is discreetly masked by a partition as she limbers up.)

INTERVIEWER. While Mrs. Treplatchly prepares herself . . . the surprise is not just hers. . . . Earlier this evening, unknown to Mrs. Treplatchly, we put through a call to Mao Tse-tung in Peking . . .

(DIRECTOR /played by Mr. Williams/ and PRODUCTION ASSISTANT /played by Mr. Vernon/ appear with clipboards, and stand consulting, with a view to winding this up and going on to something else.)

INTERVIEWER. . . . and asked him if there was anything in particular, that, as representative of the People's Republic of China, he would like her to sympathize with him about. His first words were encouraging. "It's a funny thing you should ask that," he said . . .

DIRECTOR. I think we can wind this one up now.

INTERVIEWER. Oh. Right. I'll just . . . while you're setting up. (Scene changing goes on as INTERVIEWER comes down to finish what he has to say while it goes on. Others disperse and change.) . . . the upshot of it being, to cut a long story short, that Madame Mao's own personal copy of the Little Red Book . . . containing marginal notes in Mao Tse-tung's own hand . . . notes which, once incorporated into the main body of the work, could, in his own words, have been chanted in high-pitched unison throughout the length and breadth of China to the ultimate betterment of all mankind . . . had suffered a small accident. It seems that Madame Mao had taken it with her to read in the . . . (He leaves it unsaid.) and it had slipped out of her hand and down the . . . (He leaves it unsaid.) with the result that . . . advanced type of plumbing which is the glory of Chinese technology and flushes automatically the moment you get up off the seat . . .

BLACKOUT

Scene 8

LIGHTS come up on the reception room of Universal Prayer and Sympathy Services Limited. It is smooth, glossy, sleek, deep-carpeted. The whole place reeks of expensive smarm. Decor black and cream with ecclesiastical overtones. The RECEPTIONIST (played by Miss Hughes) wears a creamy white nun's habit, expensively designed to make her look as dishy as possible. She has a hushed manner, discreet air, hostessy approach.

RECEPTIONIST (on the telephone). Universal Prayer and Sympathy Services Limited. May I help you? . . . No - this is not the World Prayer Centre, but we do work in close conjunction with them. . . . Yes - well, three thousand nuns on their knees within seconds of receiving your call is certainly what they claim, and of course, being in constant touch by computer with religious bodies all over the world . . . Yes. . . . Well, if you'd care to give some particulars, Mrs. Broadbent.

(MRS. DUBARGE /played by Sybil/ enters and crosses with MR. BURBAGE /played by Mr. Williams/. They are followed by MRS. WHITBRACE.)

MRS. DUBARGE. We've become, as you probably know, part of an American-based consortium, and a good many changes will have taken place here, I expect, since Mrs. Treplatchly was the guiding spirit. (They exit.)

RECEPTIONIST (still into the telephone). You'll be

conversant, I expect, with our scale of charges, which is five guineas an hour for the first hour in the case of both prayer and sympathy, after which prices do start to rise rather steeply, I'm afraid. . . . Not at all. An hour's intensive prayer and sympathy is an awful lot, actually - more than it sounds. . . . Oh, ample. Ample. . . . Yes. Right away. Good-bye.

(RECEPTIONIST exits as MRS. DUBARGE and MR. BURBAGE re-enter and cross,followed by MRS. WHITBRACE.)

MRS. DUBARGE. Prayer as well, oh yes. But we haven't parted company with our origins. We keep up our traditions, Mr. Burbage.

BURBAGE. This is what? A training session, I take it.

(Lights go up on a TRAINEE /played by Miss Hughes/. TRAINEE has cushions strapped on like a Mae West, and is miming Mr. Whitbrace bobbing about in the water.)

MRS. DUBARGE. Yes. She's learning to identify with the prospective sympathee. Which in this case, of course, is . . . naturally . . . the man of the moment, that they all come in here mad keen to sympathize with . . .

BURBAGE. Yes. I can see.

MRS. DUBARGE. We give them a choice of audition pieces, but it's nearly always - "Oh, Mrs. Dubarge, do let me identify with Mr. Whitbrace!"

BURBAGE. She seems to be shaping rather well.

MRS. DUBARGE. Very well indeed, for a beginner. She's obviously sympathized with somebody before.

BURBAGE. What, in your experience, is the best time of the day for sympathizing? Before breakfast . . . ?

MRS. DUBARGE. Oh, any time at all. That's just an old wives' tale that sympathy felt before breakfast is worth its weight in gold. The important thing is that it should get out to the person or persons it's meant for, and so often it doesn't. Either it goes to the wrong person, or it simply vanishes into thin air. And it's quite unnecessary. It's purely and simply a matter of technique . . . learning how to project it properly . . . and the secret of that is identify, identify, identify . . . first, last and all the time.

(They exit as MRS. BLITHEHAMPTON /played by Miss Stewart/, Trainee Supervisor, enters and speaks to TRAINEE.)

MRS. BLITHEHAMPTON. Yes, I've been watching you, and I think we're making progress. You're obviously with him in your mind, but the physical manifestations need a little more zing to them. . . . (TRAINEE tries to put more zing into it.) That's right. And your arms . . . flap those about a little bit. . . . Yes. . . . Gasp for air as you inadvertently go under for a moment. . . . Good. . . . Keep those arms flapping. . . . Not too . . . that's better. . . . Good. (TRAINEE takes a breather.) Yes, that was very good, but you must be warned against the danger of getting carried away in the enthusiasm of the moment.

TRAINEE. Yes. I overdid it a bit.

MRS. BLITHEHAMPTON. You're feeling it, aren't you? Under here.

TRAINEE. Yes, I am rather.

MRS. BLITHEHAMPTON. It's one of the first things you must guard against. If you dislocate your elbow, it's virtually impossible to sympathize with anybody properly - it's very painful, and you need every scrap of sympathy you can spare for yourself. You can end up on a stretcher, and once that happens you're out of the race completely for the next six weeks so far as showing sympathy is concerned.

TRAINEE. Yes, I'll try and remember that. Shall I . . .

MRS. BLITHEHAMPTON. Yes. Enthusiasm, but in moderation.

(TRAINEE and MRS. BLITHEHAMPTON exit as MRS. DUBARGE comes into reception room with MR. BURBAGE. They are accompanied by MRS. WHITBRACE.)

MRS. DUBARGE. And of course if he's never been sympathized with under an awning, it's quite an experience.

BURBAGE. I can imagine.

MRS. DUBARGE. It's a scheme which we've devised fairly recently for people in Mrs. Whitbrace's situation . . . who want basically to do their own sympathizing, but feel more confident if they can do it in the company of others, and with one or two trained operators on hand to help and advise them if necessary.

BURBAGE. How would it . . . ?

MRS. DUBARGE. What we would do would be to send Mrs. Whitbrace out with a party . . . perhaps seven or eight people intent, like yourself, on sympathizing with a loved one in misfortune . . .

MRS. WHITBRACE. Yes.

MRS. DUBARGE. Together with a sprinkling of

our own helpers . . . and send them all out with hampers somewhere . . . or on one of our own launches down the river, and you would do your sympathizing over a specially prepared buffet lunch.

BURBAGE (to MRS. WHITBRACE). That sounds . . .

MRS. WHITBRACE. Yes, it does.

MRS. DUBARGE. There'd be absolutely no difference of course in the depth or quality of the basic sympathy shown . . . but . . . champagne, strawberries . . . it does just serve to give that added touch of poignancy to the situation . . . and of course the thoughts winging out to him are perhaps that little bit more acceptable for being tinged with a modicum of high living . . . which is something he can share with you in his thoughts as he bobs up and down . . . and enjoy by proxy while at the same time knowing that he's not forgotten. So . . . let's go along, shall we, to the office, and we can make all the necessary arrangements.

MRS. WHITBRACE. Is it going to cost very much?

MRS. DUBARGE. Oh, I think Mr. Whitbrace is sufficient of a world celebrity by now to qualify for . . . (To MR. BURBAGE.) don't you?

BURBAGE. Oh, yes.

MRS. DUBARGE. On the house. (The telephone rings.) Oh. Excuse me. (She picks up the telephone and speaks into it.) Prayer, yes. . . . Well, if it's something comparatively small and easy to handle, there are, of course, the Little Sisters of the Resurrection who come out remarkably well in "Which?" but . . . Saint Who? . . . Saint Anastasius. . . . On the other hand, I think I should warn you that not all the saints are equally on the ball when it comes to gaining the ear of the Almighty. With eternity in front of them, they tend to have a less than total sense of urgency. They're working to a totally different timescale, you see, and if your Aunt Maude's fallen down a crevasse in Mexico, she would probably appreciate divine intervention in her own lifetime. . . . Yes. . . . Yes. . . . Excuse me one moment. . . .

(RECEPTIONIST enters and hands MRS. DUBARGE a message.)

RECEPTIONIST. About Mr. . . .

MRS. DUBARGE. Oh. That puts things rather back in the melting pot. (She addresses herself to MR. BURBAGE.) It seems that Mr. Whitbrace . . . by some mishap which is not at the moment clear . . . has . . . been knocked unconscious.

BURBAGE. Unconscious?

MRS. DUBARGE (hands him memo). No details, but . . .

MRS. WHITBRACE. Oh, no. Not unconscious. It's the one thing he's always dreaded. He's always dreaded he'd be knocked unconscious. He used to lie awake dreaming about it.

RECEPTIONIST. Perhaps . . .

MRS. DUBARGE. Yes. (RECEPTIONIST shepherds MRS. WHITBRACE out.)

BURBAGE. I think this had better be followed up. (He exits.)

MRS. DUBARGE. We shall have to re-think things a little bit. No point in trying to foist sympathy on to an unconscious man. (Into telephone.) Hallo . . . Hallo! . . .

BLACKOUT

Scene 9

LIGHTS come up on the Ship's lounge in which we see CLARENCE, SYBIL, MRS. CRABBE-HARMSWORTH, BAVERSTOCK.

MRS. CRABBE-HARMSWORTH. A lifebelt . . . ? (Pause.)

CLARENCE. Just at the very moment when rescue was beginning to seem as far away as ever. (Pause.)

MRS. CRABBE-HARMSWORTH. How did it . . . ?

BAVERSTOCK. Some busybodying idiot up on deck. Saw it there, and . . .

SYBIL(from paper). "Struck him on the side of the head as he was shaking some water out of his ear."

MRS. CRABBE-HARMSWORTH. Just how utterly cynical and irresponsible can you get? (Pause.)

BAVERSTOCK. Interesting study. What a man's motives are for that sort of thing.

CLARENCE. Complex workings of the human mind. (Pause.) No light weight - receive one of those full on the cranium.

BAVERSTOCK. And yet you can't, I suppose, blame the lifebelt.

CLARENCE. Use it's put to.

BAVERSTOCK. In and of itself, it's a neutral thing. Neither good nor bad. Gets into the wrong hands. That's when the trouble starts. Some woolly-minded do-gooder with an I. Q. of zero. Thinks all you've got to do to put the world to rights overnight is to go out and fling a lifebelt at the first drowning man you see.

SYBIL. If only it <u>were</u> that easy!

(PUTNEY enters with later editions of the papers, and hands them around.)

PUTNEY. All speaking with one mind for a change.

SYBIL (reading from paper). "This deplorable and foolhardy act . . . brings into disrepute the genuine efforts being made on behalf of the drowning man." I should think it did.

BAVERSTOCK (reading from paper). "Wicked jape that could cost a life . . . high time to introduce more stringent regulations . . . "

MRS. CRABBE-HARMSWORTH (reading from paper). "The lesson will not, one hopes, be lost on those in authority."

CLARENCE (reading from paper). "Until every life-belt is safely under lock and key, no means must be ignored that holds out the slightest hope of preventing a recurrence of this sort of tragic incident, even if this means introducing - for the first time on shipboard - the much maligned breathalyser." (Pause.)

BAVERSTOCK. One too many.

CLARENCE. Seem so.

BAVERSTOCK. Begins to make sense. (Pause.)

MRS. CRABBE-HARMSWORTH. I suppose one's hardly surprised. It had that sort of ring to it from the start. (Pause.)

BAVERSTOCK. Temperance lobby out in force, I suppose.

MRS. CRABBE-HARMSWORTH. Oh, yes. Manna from heaven. (Pause.)

SYBIL. It's a puzzle how it was allowed to happen. Someone, surely, must have noticed what state he was in the moment he went up on deck.

BAVERSTOCK. Quite.

CLARENCE. Restraining hand.

BAVERSTOCK. Done with tact and no feathers ruffled.

SYBIL. Instead of which . . .

MRS. CRABBE-HARMSWORTH. Quite. (PUTNEY

switches on transistor radio.)

VOICE (from radio). . . . after a lengthy struggle was eventually overpowered, and will appear at Bow Street tomorrow charged with misdemeanor on the high seas. Other news items . . . (PUTNEY switches off, and goes out. Pause.)

SYBIL. So what are his chances?

CLARENCE. Anybody's guess. (Pause.)

MRS. CRABBE-HARMSWORTH. Slim, I should think. You don't survive long with a concussion in a heavy sea. (Pause.)

SYBIL. Should we . . . ?

CLARENCE. Yes. It might be a nice thought.

SYBIL. Petition the authorities for a wreath in the event that . . .

MRS. CRABBE-HARMSWORTH. Yes. A round robin, or something of that kind.

BAVERSTOCK. Least we can do, I think. (Pause. No one makes the smallest move.)

CLARENCE. Oh. Seems we've been forestalled.

(PUTNEY enters with wreath in form of ship's lifebelt. The name "S. S. Bay of Naples" is picked out of it in flowers. In the middle, a large black-bordered card with a message written on it.)

PUTNEY. Hope it isn't premature.

BAVERSTOCK. In the form of a lifebelt.

PUTNEY. It seemed fitting.

CLARENCE (reading from card). "World National Help-You-Out Year Week Special Appeals Campaign. . . . Deepest Sympathy."

BAVERSTOCK. I think we can all endorse that. (PUTNEY takes the wreath around for individual inspection. Each puts flower in buttonhole or pins to dress.) Lowered into the water.

MRS. CRABBE-HARMSWORTH. Yes. I think it should.

CLARENCE. At the appropriate moment.

(MISS HAVERGAL enters.)

MISS HAVERGAL. Is he . . . ?

SYBIL. Not yet. We're waiting for something to come through. (Pause.) One can't believe he's all but gone. (Pause.)

CLARENCE. Be like treading on a stair that isn't there for a time. 'Til it wears off. (Pause.)

BAVERSTOCK. All come to it, I suppose. Sooner or later. (Pause.)

CLARENCE. That or something else. (Pause.)

MRS. CRABBE-HARMSWORTH. Irony it should have happened now. Just at the very moment when we're coming up to the anniversary.

SYBIL. The anniversary?

MRS. CRABBE-HARMSWORTH. It's a whole year, you know.

SYBIL. It can't be!

MRS. CRABBE-HARMSWORTH. It was a whole year more than eighteen months ago. We should have had the celebrations then but for delays in getting it organized. And now that it has come, he won't be there to take part . . . except perhaps in spirit . . . if he can be induced to breathe his last in time. (They begin to regroup for a public commemorative meeting dedicated to Albert Whitbrace as the Founder-Hero of the Albert Whitbrace Foundation.)

SYBIL. It's hard to believe it's a whole year.

CLARENCE. Let alone two and a half.

SYBIL. It seems like yesterday.

BAVERSTOCK. The least we can do, I suppose, is to pay a tribute both to the man, and to what the man has come to represent to the world at large in this day of unrest and disillusionment . . .

(NOTE: The statements which follow have begun to take on the character of public utterances made independently of each other, but overlapping, and with certain words and phrases spoken in chorus by one or more of the other characters present.)

CLARENCE. We are more than happy at the way things have turned out. It has been a shot in the arm not only for Meditours Ltd., but a frankly enormous fillip to the tourist industry generally . . . which has done more to put the Bay of Naples on the map than anything we could possibly have hoped for in our wildest dreams.

PUTNEY. And which has been eminently worthwhile in every way, and has paid for itself in terms of favorable publicity for the project a hundred times over.

MISS HAVERGAL. May I add my small mite here to say that the Whitbrace saga as we know it is surely not something that should be allowed to vanish into the limbo of forgotten things, and to this end one would like to press for some concrete reminder to be instituted, in the form of a special commemorative buoy in gay and arresting colors . . . to be set up at the spot where he entered the water and was to spend so many long months . . . and moored there in perpetuity so that future generations, as they come upon it, in the dark, may pause and give thought to what it so inadequately represents.

BAVERSTOCK. We should perhaps pay tribute at this time as well to the many people whose hard work and devotion has made this great occasion possible . . . to the engineers, the lawyers, the philanthropists of every shade of pigmentation who have banded together to make the Albert Whitbrace Scheme a success . . . and not least to the dedicated but largely unsung backroom boffins whose efforts have insured that his cries for help have been heard all over the world.

MRS. CRABBE-HARMSWORTH. But in particular for the man at the center of it all, but for whose efforts there would have been no cries for the technicians to amplify . . .

CLARENCE. . . . who is unfortunately missing on this great celebratory occasion, but to whom our thoughts now turn.

SYBIL. It is a source of wonder and admiration how he has managed to fit so much in and yet at the same time set aside the necessary precious minutes so unfailingly each day throughout the whole of his ordeal to shout . . . and to go on shouting . . . so nobly and so effectively for help. Others have done so in the past . . . others will assuredly do so again in the future . . . but none more ringingly or with a more single-minded sense of purpose than the man who has been such an inspiration to us all during this testing time . . . the man at the center of all the wonderful things that have been happening all over the world these last twenty months. . . . Albert Aloysius Franklin Whitbrace!

(They revert to their former characters. Brief pause, scratching sound, loud click, and background noises as loudspeaker comes alive. Two-tone chime. Air hostessy voice. Tone suitably hushed, but otherwise matter of fact, as though giving information about the weather.)

VOICE. Passengers may like to be informed that Albert Whitbrace . . . whose plight, during the twenty-seven and a half months he has been almost continuously in the water, has caught the imagination of the public in all parts of the world . . . has now gone under for the last time. He was forty-seven. (Click.)

(Silence as they begin to disperse and MRS. WHITBRACE enters in black.)

CLARENCE. Well. So there it is.
BAVERSTOCK. Ashes to ashes. (Pause.)
CLARENCE. Had its good innings, I suppose.
BAVERSTOCK. Sort of thing that happens to all of us. Sooner or later.
CLARENCE. True.
BAVERSTOCK. That, or something else. (Pause.)
SYBIL. Was he anyone?
MRS. CRABBE-HARMSWORTH. No. I don't think he was, fortunately. (Pause.)
PUTNEY. One thing about it. Gives people a chance to do something they couldn't have done before.
CLARENCE. What's that?
PUTNEY. Collect for his widow. (Brief nod.)
CLARENCE. Everything has its bright side.
PUTNEY. Yes.
CLARENCE. Take the trouble to look for it.

(MRS. WHITBRACE remains on stage conscious of having now become the first lady of widowhood.)

BLACKOUT

NOTES ON CHARACTERS, COSTUMES AND PROPERTIES

SET:
There is an upstage ramp running across the stage from side to side. It is used as required to represent various localities, but in general for action which is going on elsewhere simultaneously with the main action. Downstage of the ramp is the main acting area.

GENERAL PROPERTIES:
Scene One: Small nondescript room in a house which has been converted into a one-man office with a trestle table (on table: pamphlets, tape recorder, telephone) and other paraphernalia appropriate to a small home-based campaign that is beginning to expand. There is a poster in the room that reads: "National Help-You-Out Year Week." The tape recorder on the table has a tape of sound effects: loud cry, huge splash, shout of "man overboard!" This tape will be played twice.

Scene Two: Small luxury cruise liner: Upstage is a ship's rail. Visible on the rail is "S.S. Bay of Naples" on a lifebelt. There is a view across the blue sea to the Bay of Naples. We hear sounds of water lapping and ropes gently straining and creaking; occasionally the cry of seagulls. Downstage is the ship's dining room with typical tables and chairs. There is a practical porthole. Menus and copies of *The Times* are on the tables.

Scene Three: Committee Room: Chairs for those in room to sit, probably around a large table. On table in front of each chair is a memorandum. Upstage is a desk with a telephone on it and papers. A wall map is on wall behind desk.

Scene Four: Ship's lounge: Comfortable chairs, a porthole window as in ship's dining room. We will hear some bars of Mendelssohn's "Wedding March" when called for in script.

Scene Five: A modern office: A large wall map (on wall) covered with small red flags. Mr. Whitbrace's position is marked by a large gold star. There is also a wall chart next to map, in the form of a giant calendar, labeled "Albert Whitbrace Scheme." Days are marked off on it to signify how long he has been in the water. Posters such as the following, are all over the room:

"World National Help-You-Out Year Week Special Appeals Campaign: Much has been done--much remains to be done. Will you help?"

"No man need be an island!"

"Do you know someone in trouble? Help us to help him help himself during World National Help-You-Out Year Week! And win a free trip for two to the Bay of Naples!"

"Buy it now! Cries for help through the ages!"

There are two office desks and chairs in the room. Each desk has a telephone on it and one also has a typewriter with paper in it.

Scene Six: Cabinet Room: Two chairs. Upstage, a huge wall map. A practical window.

Scene Seven: Ship's Lounge: Sounds of Beethoven's Fifth Piano Concerto. Comfortable chairs; a porthole window as in ship's dining room in Scene Two. Television equipment is brought in upstage, by some of the stage crew, where indicated in script, also a throne-like chair upstage and a chair for the interviewer. A partition is near by so that it can be quickly put in front of Mrs. Treplatchly when called for in the script.

Scene Eight: Reception Room of Universal Prayer and Sympathy Services Limited. It is smooth, glossy sleek, deep-carpeted. The whole place reeks of expensive smarm. Decor, black and cream with ecclesiastical overtones. The receptionist desk has a telephone on it.

Scene Nine: Ship's lounge: Same as in Scene Seven, but without the piano music. There is a transistor radio somewhere in the lounge.

CHARACTERS:

MR. WILLIAMS: In his late forties. He also plays Mr. Burbage, Clarence, Archbishop, Cabinet Minister, and T.V. Director.

Scene One: Wears overcoat; later takes it off and hangs it up. He carries letters.

Scene Six: As Cabinet Minister: Telegrams.

Scene Seven: As T.V. Director: Clipboard.

MR. VERNON: In his early forties. He also plays Mr. Baverstock, Senior Civil Servant, Mr. Clapton, Piano Engineer, Production Assistant.

Scene Six: As Senior Civil Servant: Telegrams.

Scene Seven: As Production Assistant: Clipboard.

MR. PUTNEY: In his late twenties. He also plays the Steward, Junior Civil Servant, Solicitor, Trade Union Leader, Lawyer, Interviewer.

Scene Two: Notebook and pencil.

Scene Six: As Lawyer: Telephone, a thesis, a pointer to indicate a specific section on the map.

Scene Seven: As Interviewer: A book containing the life story of Mrs. Treplatchly, including a framed testimonial bestowed upon Mrs. Treplatchly by the Biafrans out of gratitude for her sympathizing with them in 1970. This is flashed up as if on a screen as if television audiences were viewing it.

Scene Nine: Several newspapers; a wreath in the form of a lifebelt, with the name "S.S. Bay of Naples" picked out of it in flowers. In the middle, a large black-bordered card with a message written on it.

SYBIL: In her middle forties. She also plays Miss Rugg, Mrs. Clacton, Mrs. Treplatchly, Mrs. Dubarge.
Scene Two: Newspaper.
Scene Three: As Miss Rugg: Letter of apology, notebook and pencil.
Scene Seven: As Mrs. Treplatchly: Dressed in regal splendor. Handkerchief.
Scene Nine: Newspaper.

MISS STEWART: In her late thirties. She also plays Mrs. Crabbe-Harmsworth, Mrs. Carthage, Mrs. Blithehampton.

MISS HUGHES: In her twenties. She also plays Miss Havergal, Flag-Selling Lady, Miss Linthropp, Second Employee, Girl Reporter, Receptionist Nun, Trainee.
Scene Two: As Miss Havergal and Flag-Selling Lady. As Flag Seller she has flag pins on a tray, and wears a Salvation Army bonnet.
Scene Three: As Girl Reporter: Notebook and pencil.
Scene Five: As Miss Linthropp: Note.
Scene Six: As Girl Reporter: Notebook and pencil.
Scene Eight: As Receptionist Nun: Wears a creamy white nun's habit, expensively designed to make her look as dishy as possible. She should have some regular clothes (such as slacks and a blouse) under her nun's habit, so that she can quickly change into the Trainee. As Trainee she has cushions strapped on her like a Mae West. After her scene as Trainee she changes back into nun's habit and becomes Receptionist again. As Receptionist again: A written message.

MRS. WHITBRACE: In her early thirties.
Scene Three: A photograph of her husband's married sister.
Scene Nine: Dressed in black mourning clothes.

NOTE:
The properties listed above are those specifically mentioned in the script. However it is not necessary that the actual objects be used. Much (or all) of the action may be pantomimed if desired.

Switches from scene to scene should be made as rapidly as possible, so as not to leave the audience sitting in the dark after a blackout. The action should be almost continuous from scene to scene, with lights coming up in one area as they go down on another.

DIRECTOR'S NOTES

DIRECTOR'S NOTES

DIRECTOR'S NOTES

DIRECTOR'S NOTES